AWESOME ANIMALS

WONDERFUL WILDLIFE
EDITED BY ROSEANNA CASWELL

AWESOME ANIMALS - WONDERFUL WILDLIFE

WHALES

Whales can grow up to thirty metres long
Baby whales have little moustaches
Whales have balloon plates instead of teeth
A whale's tongue weighs as much as an elephant
It's the same size as a car
Whales can live up to ninety years old
Whales are blue
Humpback whales have bumpy skin
Did you know whales stay out of the water for some seconds?

Aanuoluwapo Salami (6)
All Saints CE Primary School, Wigston Magna

TIGERS

Tigers can get to 11 feet long
The cubs stay with their mother until they are 2 or 3 years old

Tigers can't purr like other cats
Tigers live in Asia

They can live up to 15 years
Some tigers eat fish

Did you know that tiger cubs learn to hunt by watching their mum?

Raavan Gajendran (6)
All Saints CE Primary School, Wigston Magna

HIPPOS

Hippos eat at night when it is cooler
Hippos can live for 40 years
Hippos spend six hours eating at night
They are nocturnal
Hippos can be found in parts of East Africa
Hippos have thick skin
They have short legs and a huge head
Hippos are herbivores
They eat plants and grass.

Kundai Kunaka (6)
All Saints CE Primary School, Wigston Magna

HIPPOS

Hippos eat grass
Hippos walk one thousand miles
Hippos have a big mouth
Hippos have yellow teeth
Hippos feed their babies milk
Hippos walk to swim
The hippo opens its mouth and eats mud
Did you know hippos have yellow teeth?

Anokh Singh (6)
All Saints CE Primary School, Wigston Magna

AWESOME ANIMALS - WONDERFUL WILDLIFE

TIGERS

Tiger cubs learn to hunt by watching
their mum
Did you know male tigers are called dogs
And the female tigers are called tigress?
Did you know tigers are called mammals?
Did you know orange tigers are summer tigers?

Antonia Maria Valeanu (6)
All Saints CE Primary School, Wigston Magna

WHALES

Blue whales are mammals
Blue whales are carnivores
They eat about four tonnes of krill a day
Did you know whales are mammals?

Kupakwashe Jakata (6)
All Saints CE Primary School, Wigston Magna

AWESOME ANIMALS - WONDERFUL WILDLIFE

TIGERS

Tigers eat meat
Tigers have sharp teeth and sharp claws
Tigers walk in the long grass
Did you know that tigers run fast?

Harley Chase Sidwell (6)
All Saints CE Primary School, Wigston Magna

WHALES

Did you know sperm whales are toothed
Orcas are actually dolphins
The orca jumps because it is looking
for food.

Hayden Jude (6)
All Saints CE Primary School, Wigston Magna

WHALES

Whales live alone or in pairs
Blue whales are mammals
Whales eat about four tonnes of krill a day.

Ellis Tompkins (6)
All Saints CE Primary School, Wigston Magna

MY FAVOURITE ANIMAL

He has teeth like some scissors
His fur is orange and black
His nose is black
His teeth are sharp and pointy
His back is curly and soft
His black tail is straight
His paws are huge
His nails are strong and sharp
His ears are huge
His arm is hard
His bum is smelly
His nose is sensitive
My favourite animal is a tiger.

Phoebe Watson (6)
Anthony Curton C of E Primary School, Walpole St Peter

AWESOME ANIMALS - WONDERFUL WILDLIFE

MY FAVOURITE ANIMAL IS A CAT

Her nose is pink
She can smell very well
Her eyes are as blue as the sky
Her paws are cute
Her fur is soft like a blanket
Her teeth are shiny like a ruby
Her roar is loud like an erupting volcano
Her head is giant like a boulder
Her claws are sharp like a pin
My favourite animal is a tiger.

Grace Rawlings (6)
Anthony Curton C of E Primary School, Walpole St Peter

MY FAVOURITE ANIMAL

His claws are sharp and pointy like a knife
His head is brown like mud
His eyes are yellow
His nose is pink and smooth
His teeth are covered in blood
His fur is soft and smelly
His paws are huge
His roar is very loud
He runs very fast
My favourite animal is a bear.

Eveline Wool (6)
Anthony Curton C of E Primary School, Walpole St Peter

MY FAVOURITE ANIMAL

Her claws are as sharp as a sword
Her head is huge like a tree
Her eyes are brown like a tree trunk
Her black nose is as wet as mud
Her teeth are as shiny as a pearl
Her fur is as soft as a feather
My favourite animal is a bear.

Ivy Dix (6)
Anthony Curton C of E Primary School, Walpole St Peter

MY FAVOURITE ANIMAL IS...

The tiger's fur is orange and black
The tiger is intelligent
The tiger is big
The tiger has sharp claws
The tiger sleeps silently
The tiger hunts its prey
The tiger roars like thunder
My favourite animal is a tiger.

Amber Carveth (6)
Anthony Curton C of E Primary School, Walpole St Peter

MY FAVOURITE ANIMAL

She has scales like a red apple
She has patterns
Her eyes are yellow, pink and blue
She is as flexible as a rubber band
She has a tongue shaped like a flag
Her tail is as long as a house
My favourite animal is a snake.

Everly Rawlings (6)
Anthony Curton C of E Primary School, Walpole St Peter

MY FAVOURITE ANIMAL

His fangs are poisonous like a snake
His eyes are terrible like a spider
His tail is long like a tree trunk
His scales are smooth like a pebble
His body is slimy like a snake
My favourite animal is a snake.

Oliver Mondey (6)
Anthony Curton C of E Primary School, Walpole St Peter

MY FAVOURITE ANIMAL

He scales around the trees
His fangs are poisonous
His tail is very, very long
His body is filled with blood
His eyes are small
His tongue is like a fork
My favourite animal is a snake.

Jack Watling (6)
Anthony Curton C of E Primary School, Walpole St Peter

MY FAVOURITE ANIMAL

He has sharp teeth
He hunts for his prey
He has black fur
He runs fast
He roars really loudly
My favourite animal is a bear.

Isaac Williams (5)
Anthony Curton C of E Primary School, Walpole St Peter

MY FAVOURITE ANIMAL

He has sharp claws
He has good eyes
He has pointy claws
He has soft fur
My favourite animal is a bear.

Cole Barsby (6)
Anthony Curton C of E Primary School, Walpole St Peter

MY FAVOURITE ANIMAL

He has sharp claws
He hunts for his prey
His fur is soft and stinky
My favourite animal is a bear.

Lewis Franklin (6)
Anthony Curton C of E Primary School, Walpole St Peter

AWESOME ANIMALS - WONDERFUL WILDLIFE

MY FAVOURITE ANIMAL

He has sharp claws
He hunts for his prey
He is soft and stinky
My favourite animal is a bear.

Levi-John Crittenden (6)
Anthony Curton C of E Primary School, Walpole St Peter

MY FAVOURITE ANIMAL IS SHERE KHAN

He has claws like lightning
He has claws like thunder
My favourite animal is a snake.

Emily Campos (6)
Anthony Curton C of E Primary School, Walpole St Peter

AWESOME ANIMALS - WONDERFUL WILDLIFE

THE LITTLE PENGUIN

One cold day in Antarctica, a little penguin was standing near the icy edge. He was called Jef. He lived with his mummy and daddy.
"Ooh," he said, "I wish I could go out of my cave. What shall I do?"
"You can't go out of the cave," said his mummy and daddy.
"You will freeze!" his daddy said.
"But..."
"No buts," his daddy said.
"Okay," Jef said, "I will stay in the cave. I love you, Mummy and Daddy."
"We love you too, darling," they said.

Martha Milne (5)
Catcott Primary School, Catcott

JONAH'S JAGUAR

Jonah's jaguar was playing in the jungle and Jonah was watching Buddy play. Jonah heard running and said to Buddy, "I heard some running." He then jumped on Buddy and said, "Yeeha!"
Buddy ran as fast as he could. Jonah said it was a tiger. "We've lost it. Phew!" Jonah said. "Good boy, Buddy. You deserve breakfast."
Buddy ate it all up. Then Jonah left Buddy in the woods but Buddy went missing. Jonah looked everywhere but Buddy was not there. Jonah was shocked.
"Where is Buddy? Oh no!"
Jonah was so upset. Suddenly, he saw black stuff. It was Buddy. Jonah ran up to Buddy.
Then Buddy had lunch. Buddy loved his lunch so much. Jonah then had his lunch with Buddy. Buddy was so happy. Jonah loved Buddy so much. Then Jonah and Buddy went to sleep.

AWESOME ANIMALS - WONDERFUL WILDLIFE

Buddy woke up Jonah. Jonah then got some breakfast and Buddy too. Then Jonah let Buddy go out in the garden but Buddy squeezed through the fence. Jonah looked in the garden but Buddy was at the next-door neighbour's.
Buddy came back, had lunch and dinner and they were so tired.

Xanthe Jowett (6)
Catcott Primary School, Catcott

THE CHICKEN LAID AN EGG

Once, there was a little silver chicken and it laid a golden egg. It came out so fast that he went flying through the air. He landed on a plane and went in, He saw his house and he jumped out. He landed on his house and laid a few more golden eggs for his dinner.
The next day, he had a good breakfast and it was sports day. He was running at his full speed and won the race. After school, he went home and had dinner.

Freddy Wilson (6)
Catcott Primary School, Catcott

AWESOME ANIMALS - WONDERFUL WILDLIFE

SAM'S PIG

Sam had a pig
The pig was blue
The pig was big
He lived in the box
He looked at the sun
Why did he look at the sky?
Then he saw a spooky castle
He went inside
He saw a ghost
He ran out
The sky was dark
He went to his car
Oh no, it was broken
How would he get home?
He had to walk home
He made it home.

Conor Heffernan (6)
Catcott Primary School, Catcott

BERNIE'S LIFE

Once upon a time, there was a dog called Bernie. He loved playing tug of war with me. Every day, instead of sleeping in his bed, he slept with my parents. I loved playing with my dog. Bernie is three and he is very playful. In dog years, he would be 21. Bernie loves me and I love him. I took him to the Armed Forces Day and he loved it, like me.

Elizabeth Perfect-Porter (6)
Catcott Primary School, Catcott

AWESOME ANIMALS - WONDERFUL WILDLIFE

GOAT NUMBER 2

Number 2 is super soft, small and cute
He likes to snuggle in my bedroom
He can jump so high
He can jump over electric fences
Goats are extraordinary and clever
We can shake hands and he loves me so much
When he grows up he will be really big.

Rufus Graham (6)
Catcott Primary School, Catcott

BUBBER, MY BEST FRIEND

Once upon a time, Lily had a fluffy toy animal called Bubber. Bubber was her favourite toy. One night, he went on an adventure without Lily knowing. He went to the jungle.
The next day, Lily woke up and saw he was gone. She was very upset.

Lily Carter (6)
Catcott Primary School, Catcott

MY DOG

Rex, the dog is white and fluffy
I love him
He is my favourite dog
We have lots of cuddles
He eats tripe
"Yummy!" said Rex
"Yucky," said Reggie.

Reggie Ball (6)
Catcott Primary School, Catcott

ROSIE, MY DOG

Rosie is really cute
She is a little bit large
And has fluffy blonde fur
She likes to eat chicken
And playing with Bella the cat
Rosie likes to run and bounce outside.

Darcey Solman (6)
Catcott Primary School, Catcott

JESSIE, MY FRIEND

Jessie is my dog
I really love her
Jessie is really soft and black
She loves to eat bacon and dog food
She wags her tail when she is happy
She makes me happy too.

Ewan Cairns (6)
Catcott Primary School, Catcott

I LOVE TOBY

My dog, called Toby, went to the shop to buy me a rug and some food and trees. I love him so much. When he came home we went for a walk.

Angus Crawford (6)
Catcott Primary School, Catcott

MY DOG, REGGIE

My dog, Reggie, was all alone
He ate cheese on the table at home
But he's a good boy
And I love him so much

My dog, Reggie, barks in his sleep
He makes a funny noise that goes *peep, peep, peep*
But he's a good boy
And I love him so much

My dog, Reggie, is in the park
When a dog comes close, he goes *bark, bark, bark*
But he's a good boy
And I love him so much.

Lois Burt-Fahy (6)
Christ Church CE Primary School, Lambeth

THE BUNNIES AND THE LION

One day, there was a little bunny called Alicia who went to the forest. She loved the forest because she had other friends. They liked ten games. They were away together when there was a lion that wanted to eat them all. The bunny was too fast for the lion. The bunny was safe.

Alicia Diaz-Mauriño Padial (6)
Christ Church CE Primary School, Lambeth

SMALL BUT FAST

Once upon a time, in the deep blue sea, there was a huge whale as big as a dinosaur could be.
There was also a tiny shrimp, chased by a shaking shark and the big whale watched the chase across the sand.
The tiny shrimp scrambled away, escaping from the shark again.

David Titcu (6)
Christ Church CE Primary School, Lambeth

WILD HEROES MAKING NOISE

Once upon a time, there was a band. It was a cat band called Wild Heroes. The band had two rules:
Rule number 1: Cats only
Rule number 2: No loud instruments.
The band were famous for their amazing song 'Scaredy Cat'. The band was so famous they all became rich. The band toured all over the world. They played in Europe, Asia, Africa, North and South America and Australia. They even played for the king.
The lead of the band, Atticus, was extremely happy. Atticus and the band hadn't always been so famous. Before Wild Heroes got together, Atticus had another life, but that's another story...
Atticus wanted to win a Cattitude Superstar trophy. They were going to have to put on their best performance ever!
Soon, the day came. The Wild Heroes went on stage and played their song. The crowd went wild. They chanted, "Wild Heroes! Wild Heroes!"
Miss Poodle Pot, the mayor, was the judge. She was hard to impress. Miss Poodle Pot decided the winners would be... The Howling Hounds!

What! The Wild Heroes came second. The crowd still chanted, "Wild Heroes!"
Atticus and the band weren't disappointed. The crowd left and the band packed their instruments and their van to set off on the next adventure.
A few weeks later, Atticus turned 56. He decided he was going to retire. Wild Heroes looked for a new leader. Oscar from The Miaowowswers is joining the band. Atticus will have front-row tickets for their next concert.

Lily Watson (7)
Dinnington First School, Dinnington Village

MRS POLLY PEARL

Mrs Polly Pearl was a teacher. She was a strict teacher but she let them have extra playtime. But she never helped them with spelling. They had to write the word 'temperature' and stuff like that. She was nice by getting the class a caterpillar. They wanted it to turn into a pupa. When the pupa hatched it had turned into an amazing, beautiful butterfly.

The class and Mrs Polly Pearl released the butterfly on the playground. It flew off to find some colourful flowers so it could eat some nectar. I knew it would have somewhere safe to sleep because the school had a lovely patch of grass and flowers so the butterfly would be able to sleep under the flower petals or hide in the long grass. The butterfly would lay its eggs on a leaf or flower and the lifecycle would start again and again. Suddenly, Mrs Polly Pearl shouted, "Everybody back to class!"

We all groaned because we knew it was time for maths!

Olivia Hutchison (7)
Dinnington First School, Dinnington Village

AWESOME ANIMALS - WONDERFUL WILDLIFE

A DISASTER DAY AT THE ZOO

Once upon a time, there was a girl. She was going to the zoo. She packed a packed lunch. She put in a sandwich, banana, orange juice and a chocolate bar. She skipped to the zoo.

First, she saw some monkeys. While she was taking a photo, one of the monkeys took her banana! Next, she looked at the koala. While she was looking at her photo, the koala pinched the sandwich from her lunch bag.

Then it was time to see the penguins. One of them waddled by and snatched her chocolate bar. Later, she saw the zebras. One of them grabbed her juice while she wasn't looking.

Finally, it was lunchtime. The little girl sat down but there were only crumbs left. She saw a shop and a very kind zookeeper gave her a sandwich, orange, chocolate and a drink.

The girl said, "The cheeky animals have taken my food!"

The zookeeper said, "They're always doing that!"

Millie Jones (7)
Dinnington First School, Dinnington Village

THE 'PURRFECT' PET

Jerry is a black-and-white cat who is cunning beyond belief
He's definitely a ring leader, some would call him a chief
His constant meowing around the streets
Makes the neighbours think he's lost, hungry and alone
But in fact, Jerry is being wise as he has a bowl full of food at home
Inside, when no one is watching, he's soft, cuddly and purrs
But as soon as he goes out the cat flap, he always moans and grrrs
Jerry won't sleep well unless he's on my lap
He refuses to drink water unless it's running from a tap
Beware if he comes in late and you hear screeching around the house
He's decided to bring you a present of a bird or a mouse
Jerry can be annoying and sometimes needs a vet
But he's my Jerry and my 'purrfect' pet.

Emilia Umeh (7)
Dinnington First School, Dinnington Village

AWESOME ANIMALS - WONDERFUL WILDLIFE

THE ANGELFISH ADVENTURE

Angel the angelfish was as black as a jaguar. He had pointy fins like angel wings. He lived in a slow-moving river basin in the Amazon rainforest. Angel was bored of staying in the river basin and wanted to go on an adventure to the Empire State Building in New York. He had a magical map to guide the way, a packed lunch, a sleeping bag and his favourite toys.

After swimming for a while, Angel bumped into an octopus and they became best friends. Next, they saw an amazing underwater rare, awesome crystal. They were stunned. They picked it up and went back on their journey.

Later on, they saw a hammerhead shark who gave them a boost. They saw lots of fun things on the way and then they saw the stupendous Empire State Building. They decided to stay.

Madeleine Harper (7)
Dinnington First School, Dinnington Village

THE WONDERFUL UMBRELLA OCTOPUSES

Did you know that a female umbrella octopus is called a hen?
Did you know that there are 37 species of umbrella octopus?
Have you heard that umbrella octopuses live for 3-5 years?
Did you know an umbrella octopus eats shrimps, krill and other small crustaceans?
Did you know that an umbrella octopus is also known as a flapjack octopus?
Have you heard that umbrella octopuses are dark red?
Did you know that an umbrella octopus can defend themselves by curling up their tentacles to protect their body?
Did you know that female umbrella octopuses lay 100,000 eggs at a time but only a few get to become adults?
A dumbo octopus is a species from the 37.
I hope you have enjoyed learning about umbrella octopuses.

Emily Carr (7)
Dinnington First School, Dinnington Village

AWESOME ANIMALS - WONDERFUL WILDLIFE

TIGER IN LONDON

Once, there was a lonely tiger who lived in the jungle. He had no friends. Today he decided to go to London to make some friends. On the way, he met a gorilla and a monkey. They went to London. He thought it was scary because it was big.
He went to say hello but people ignored him so he made a big roar. But they still ignored him. He saw the Queen and had a cup of tea and some pavlova. He saw Paddington and he tipped his hat. He went to the London Zoo and saw his cousins Lion and Leopard. Then he saw a palace. He climbed to the top. He felt very proud and relieved. Then he saw a brown clock. It was a giant! He wondered if he could climb it so he did. He climbed and climbed and made it to the top and made a big roar!

Thomas Illingworth (7)
Dinnington First School, Dinnington Village

CHEETAH IN NEW YORK

There was a cheetah called Harry. He wanted to go on the train to New York.
He saw a library and a lady walking. The lady said, "What a strange animal, he must be a cheetah. Just ignore him."
Harry ran away from the library and saw a police station and a zoo. He saw lots of animals. Harry saw a lady who made a funny face and he ran away.
Harry ran very fast to the boat which took him to the Statue of Liberty. He saw her pretend fire. Harry got back on the boat.
Harry got back on the train and went home. He said, "What a strange city!"

Thomas Rodgers (7)
Dinnington First School, Dinnington Village

AWESOME ANIMALS - WONDERFUL WILDLIFE

THE LITTLE HAMSTER

Once upon a time, there was a hamster. Her name was Honey. Honey loved to be in the wild. She had animal friends and she had an owner.
One day, she got lost. She didn't know what had happened but her animal friends could help her. She found her house. She loved being back home. She got fed and she still loved the wild. Her friends would always be by her side.
The next day she made a friend. Her name was Amber. After that day they were besties forever and played all day long.

Evie Simpson (7)
Dinnington First School, Dinnington Village

THERE ARE ANIMALS IN THE ZOO

There are monkeys in the zoo
There are elephants too
They are both in the zoo
And they trumpet like you
With kangaroos too
They hop like you with their baby joeys too
But not like you
Zebras with stripes on their backs
Giraffes see their back
And they all start to laugh
Just like you
Now all of the animals are in the zoo
Wait, what's that sound?
Grrrrrr!
Argh! It's a tiger!

Katie Downie (6)
Dinnington First School, Dinnington Village

AWESOME ANIMALS - WONDERFUL WILDLIFE

FABULOUS FACTS OF FUN

Did you know fish can sleep with their eyes open?
An orca whale sleeps with one eye closed
Did you know dogs can smell 10,000 times better than we do?
Frogs have to come to the surface to breathe air just like us
Caterpillars can change form by making their own cocoon
This is the pupa stage and when it hatches it becomes a small beautiful butterfly
How awesome is that?

Leo T (7)
Dinnington First School, Dinnington Village

IVY'S DOG FACTS

Dogs cannot eat chocolate
Dogs can eat doggy ice cream
All puppies are born deaf
Dogs do not see colours like humans
Dogs need lots of exercise
Dogs need feeding at least 2 times a day
Play with your dog so it doesn't get bored
Train your dog
Your dog can smell 40 times more than you
Your dog has dreams.

Ivy Whitelaw (7)
Dinnington First School, Dinnington Village

MY FAVOURITE ANIMAL

R abbits are soft and fuzzy
A rabbit jumps really high
B ut they run away from predators
B aby rabbits are called kits
I wish I could have a pet rabbit
T hey like to eat carrots
S ome live in burrows and some live in hutches.

Olivia Imrie (7)
Dinnington First School, Dinnington Village

I LIKE TO BLEND IN

I would like to be a praying mantis
Because I would have 5 eyes to see everything...
What about a yellow crab spider?
I could camouflage in the yellow dandelions or sunflowers
So I could catch a bee and take it to my spiderweb!

Better to be a chameleon
I could camouflage against anything
Even on you!

Imagine if I was a Jesus lizard...
I could be the only creature that can run on water

If I was a crocodile
I would blend in with the dirty green water and catch my prey

I would like to be a jaguar
Because he has the strongest bite of any other animal except poisonous snakes

To be a cobra snake would be cool
I would charm the king but also have venom

I can be a tiger too
And camouflage in the leaves when the prey is close by

I would like to be a lion, the king of
the savannah
They can camouflage in the sable-coloured grass
And roar when there are things close by
You can hear me roar from Africa!

Raen Akaal Singh Gill (5)
Durston House School, Ealing

AWESOME ANIMALS

Giraffes are very heavy and tall
And mice are very light and small

Monkeys are very funny
And bees make honey

Manatees are shy -
They hide when someone comes by!

Elephants have trunks
And camels have humps

Pangolins have tough scales
And long tails

Koalas and joeys sleep all day
But kangaroos hop, jump and play!

Arjun Paranjpe (5)
Durston House School, Ealing

PEACOCK

The peacock is big and colourful
The peacock is beautiful
The peacock is cute and interesting
The peacock's eyes are glittering
The peacock is cool
The peacock has nice patterns on its feathers
The peacock spreads its tail
The peacock looks quite amazing.

Amelia Williams (7)
Greenacres Primary School, Harlescott Grange

ALL ABOUT SNAKES

Snakes are strong and fast to catch
their prey
Snakes make circles to sleep
Snakes have a venomous bite
Snakes are black and all sorts of colours
Snakes are shiny in the dark
Snakes are aggressive to bite animals
Snakes are reptiles because they are scaly.

Liam Idahosa (7)
Greenacres Primary School, Harlescott Grange

KOALA

The koala is small and soft
The koala is kind and harmless
The koala can climb the tree
The koala eats lots of food
The koala eats lunch, supper and breakfast
The koala is soft and green
The koala is lovely
The koala has small paws.

Kacie-Mabel Bates (6)
Greenacres Primary School, Harlescott Grange

DOG

The dog is brown
He has a dripping tongue
His tongue hangs from his mouth
He runs really fast
He swings his tail
He has a really loud bark.

Finley Weston (6)
Greenacres Primary School, Harlescott Grange

CAT

The cat is nice, black and fluffy
The cat has green eyes and a pink nose
The cat has thin whiskers
The cat has sharp claws to help it climb trees.

Kiara Austin (7)
Greenacres Primary School, Harlescott Grange

PONY

There was a pony that was fluffy and cute but he was lonely. He was brown, white, shy and slow. He lived on a farm. He liked to play in the meadow.

Zoe Lowe (6)
Greenacres Primary School, Harlescott Grange

BUTTERFLY

The butterfly has wings
The butterfly is little
The butterfly flies in the sky
The butterfly lands on their home far away.

Archie Scoyne-Nicholls (5)
Greenacres Primary School, Harlescott Grange

FOX

The fox is orange
The fox has sharp teeth
The fox has crinkly ears
The fox has a fluffy tail
The fox can run fast.

Summer Thomas (6)
Greenacres Primary School, Harlescott Grange

MY DOG

My dog is called Bruce
He always plays catch
He is grey and soft
He is friendly and slow
He always barks loudly.

Amelia Spooner (7)
Greenacres Primary School, Harlescott Grange

AXOLOTL

Axolotls are cute and kind
They are colourful
They can be pink
I like them because they're cute.

Rosa Leigh (6)
Greenacres Primary School, Harlescott Grange

MONKEYS

Monkeys are fast
Monkeys are brown
They are strong and happy.

Teddy Clarke (6)
Greenacres Primary School, Harlescott Grange

THE EVIL MAN'S DINNER PLAN

Once upon a time, there lived a cat named Seth. Seth was a smart cat but some evil fish weren't scared of the cat, even though cats eat fish. The fish wanted to eat Seth for breakfast, brunch, lunch and dinner. The two fish, named Robin and Din Din, wanted to eat the cat.

The next day the cat was gone. An evil man had taken Seth. The evil man took Seth to his evil lair. The mean man ate the cat for supper and Seth didn't exist anymore.

Robin and Din Din were really upset because they hadn't eaten in days and they had wanted him to themselves. The evil man gave them a crumb but that wasn't enough because they were still hungry and so was the rest of the fish. The fish thought of an idea... Revenge!

They gathered weapons and swam to the evil man's lair using their fins to release arrows. They hit the evil man's lair and everything went dark. The man got very angry and got revenge so he ate his own fish and they never existed ever again. The evil man sat in his amazing lair with his belly full and a smirk on his face.

Lennox Kennedy (7)
Grove Vale Primary School, Great Barr

MARVELLOUS, MISCHIEVOUS MOLLY

My nan used to live by herself which made me feel quite sad. Then one day she introduced us to Molly, her crazy four-legged friend. Molly is adorable. She has silky brown fur as soft as a cloud.
Now my nan has company, she can talk to Molly and take her for long peaceful walks in the park. Me and my brother are allergic to dogs so we can't have one live in our home. However, we can join my nan and Molly for walks and we laugh loudly when Molly hops like a bunny along the soft yellow path.
There are lots of reasons why I love Molly. She is energetic, tiny, cuddly and cheeky. She has small floppy ears that blow like flags in the wind. The main reason I adore Molly is because she makes my nan feel special and happy and she no longer lives on her own.

Evie Bayliss (7)
Grove Vale Primary School, Great Barr

ALL ABOUT PANDAS

Pandas have distinctive black and white fur around their eyes and on their ears, legs and shoulders
Their thick, woolly fur keeps them warm in their cool mountain homes
The name panda is used for two mammals that live in Asia; the giant panda and the red panda
Despite their similar name, the two are not scientifically related.
Giant pandas are loved because of their unique eyes
Giant pandas are mainly found in China
Giant pandas love to roll forward, backwards and even sideways
Pandas are overall pretty lazy animals
Pandas are known to be clumsy because of their round body and short limbs, making them easily fall off things, balance and roll
Pandas happily love to eat bamboo.

Zara Saoud (7)
Grove Vale Primary School, Great Barr

AWESOME ANIMALS - WONDERFUL WILDLIFE

THE LION

Once upon a time, a lion named Leo lived in a forest. He lived with his mother.
One day, his mum said, "Time for supper!"
He went downstairs but couldn't find his mother. He realised it was barbecue day, so he went outside.
He still couldn't find his mother. He thought she was finding some more meat but then he found a snake eating her supper. He was so scared that he tried to run away.
Suddenly, a shark with powers came to save Leo the lion. He was like a megalodon. He was as fast as Pikachu. Then a jellyfish came and scared Leo the lion.
After, he found his mother in the forest.

Aryan Mall (7)
Grove Vale Primary School, Great Barr

INTERESTING FACTS ABOUT GIRAFFES

Diet
Some giraffes eat leaves, buds, trees, shrubs, herbs, climber vines, flowers
and fruit

Appearance
Over 111,000 giraffes live on Planet Earth
Male giraffes are called bulls and female giraffes are called cows
Male giraffes are 18 feet and 3,000 pounds
Female giraffes are up to 14 feet and weigh up to 1,500 pounds
Giraffes are the tallest land mammal
Males range from 16-18 feet and weigh as much as 4,2000 pounds
A cow reaches 14-16 feet

Habitat
Giraffes live in grasslands, woodlands, savannahs, Kenya and Zimbabwe.

Summer Jambwa (7)
Grove Vale Primary School, Great Barr

AWESOME ANIMALS - WONDERFUL WILDLIFE

TWOOTY THE OWL

Once upon a time, there was an owl who was separated from her parents. I bet you're wondering how. When Twooty was a baby, some gorillas destroyed their homes and trees. Twooty was the only baby who survived. It was very hard to survive. Mama Owl was telling her to fly to the highest trees.
When Twooty became a teenager, she kept on trying to find her mum but there was no sight of her. I hope she finds her mum.
She started to shout, "Mama! Mama! It's Twooty!"
When Twooty became an adult, she found her mum. It was a miracle.

Avaani Sahota (7)
Grove Vale Primary School, Great Barr

INCREDIBLE, MAGNIFICENT AND AWESOME ANIMALS

It lives in a jungle
It has brown skin
It hangs on trees
It has no hair when it is a baby
It stays with its mum and dad when it's born
It never lets go of its mum and dad
What is my animal?

Answer: A monkey!

Did you know monkeys can be fast, great at jumping and solving problems
Did you know monkeys eat plants and different types of fruit
Did you know monkeys have fingerprints like humans
For fun, monkeys like to play fight and chase each other.

Jusleen Chana (7)
Grove Vale Primary School, Great Barr

AWESOME ANIMALS - WONDERFUL WILDLIFE

THE LION IN THE ZOO

Once a lion called Kion lived in a zoo. Everyone comes to see him because he can talk.
One day, he decided to go and see the other animals. He climbed a big red wall. On the other side of the wall, it was grey. He was on the elephant's side. The elephants said hello to Kion. Kion then went over the big, grey wall.
On the other side of the wall, it was black and white. He was on the zebra side. Suddenly, Kion saw the zookeeper and ran back to the other lions and told them about his adventures.

Raina Bhatia (7)
Grove Vale Primary School, Great Barr

MY ZOO VISIT

Once I went to Twycross Zoo.
I saw a monkey looking funky.
I saw a lion whose cage was made from iron.
I saw a chimpanzee eating a banana for his tea.
I saw a tiger having fun playing in the sun.
I saw a meerkat wearing a hat.
I saw a giraffe with a funny laugh.
I saw a flamingo who was playing bingo.
I saw a zebra who was called Debra.
This was my day at the zoo.
I think you should go too!

Yuvraj Mand (7)
Grove Vale Primary School, Great Barr

GIRAFFES ARE AWESOME ANIMALS

They're friendly and they like to laugh
They have tall necks and can see far
They have long legs and can run really fast
They like eating grass and plants
Giraffes have big hearts
I'm going to have a photograph with the giraffe
You wouldn't see a giraffe in a bath
It will make you laugh
At the zoo, I saw half of the giraffes.

Zara Khan (7)
Grove Vale Primary School, Great Barr

WHAT AM I?

I have dark and light brown fur
My eye spots are under my lids
I love eating delicious bamboo
I live in the wild in the mountains of China
I'm special because there are only a few of us in the world
Most of the time I eat and sleep
What am I?

Answer: A brown/Qinling panda.

Younus Hussain (7)
Grove Vale Primary School, Great Barr

AWESOME ANIMALS - WONDERFUL WILDLIFE

GUESS MY ANIMAL

I am big, beautiful and like fish
I like to travel in pods in every ocean
They call me the largest animal on Earth
With a heart the size of a car,
A tongue as heavy as an elephant
And a voice that can be heard hundreds of kilometres away
When I go on holiday, I have a whale of a time!

Iyla Mandar (7)
Grove Vale Primary School, Great Barr

A DOG'S LOVE

Ruff! Ruff! A dog's wagging tail
Brings joy that'll never fail
With a bark, they say hello
Their love is like a warm glow

Running, playing, full of fun
Underneath the shining sun
Loyal friend through thick and thin
A dog's love is a precious win.

Evie Badger (7)
Grove Vale Primary School, Great Barr

AWESOME ANIMALS - WONDERFUL WILDLIFE

ALL ABOUT SPINOSAURUSES

What did spinosauruses eat?
We know from the shape of the dinosaur's jaws that it fed on fish.
Although it may have eaten other dinosaurs too.

Where did they live?
They lived in North Africa in the Cretaceous period.

Arjun Chana (7)
Grove Vale Primary School, Great Barr

THE RED PANDA ADVENTURE

Once upon a time, there was a group of red pandas. They were; Bambi, Bella and Bea. They loved going on adventures so much that they went every year but some of them were getting old. Luckily, the good thing was the older ones could look after the babies and the others could go on the adventure.
One day while they were clambering up a mountain, they saw a yak.
He said, "Be careful because the huntsman is coming."
The yak was right. In the middle of the night, the hunter came and put Bea in a cage.
In the morning, Bambi saw a glimpse of gold. She had found the key for Bea's cage. She saw Bea at once and set her free. She called Bella and they quickly ran away to their den.
Two years later, Bea, Bella and Bambi stayed at home and lived happily together for the rest of their lives.

Isla Young (7)
Kinross Primary School, Kinross

AWESOME ANIMALS - WONDERFUL WILDLIFE

ALL ABOUT DOGS

You need to walk your dog every day
In the morning and the evening

You need a lead for your dog
Because then it won't just run away

Play with your dog
Play toys with it
Tickle its tummy too

There are lots of different kinds of dogs
Like Westies, spaniels and Dalmatians

You need poo bags from the shop
Yes! Because you will be jailed

They eat dog food from shops like Asda and Co-Op
And all the different types of shops.

Ava Kendal-Watkins (7)
Little Dewchurch C of E Primary School, Little Dewchurch

ALL ABOUT COCKAPOOS

Cockapoos like to live with their owners
You need to get them a new toy every two months
Other times they will get bored with their toys

Food
Puppies need to be fed four times a day
An adult three times a day

How to wash your dog
To get started, you will need:
Shampoo
Flannel
Treats
Brush
Then you can start
First, rub some shampoo into your dog
Then get some water
After, you can start brushing

Types of dogs
There are lots of different dogs
Some are fluffy, some are skinny and some are spotty

AWESOME ANIMALS - WONDERFUL WILDLIFE

Dog names
Here are just some:
Cockapoos
Springer spaniels
German shepherd
Terrier

If dogs are near cats
And you bought the cat first
Keep the dog in the pen
So they get used to each other.

Jacob (7)
Little Dewchurch C of E Primary School, Little Dewchurch

SPIDER FACTS

These spiders have a dangerous thing
That could kill you, called venom
These spiders are called ambush spiders
Their size is 4-15cm
They can live in deserts, grasslands, trees and near houses

The crab spider is hard to see
Because it blends in with plants and flowers
So the animals and insects don't see them and eat them

The crab spider waits on a flower head
It will stay there for a whole day
Waiting for an insect to land on the flower.

James Cleary
Little Dewchurch C of E Primary School, Little Dewchurch

CUSTARD THE HORSE

Once upon a time, there was a horse called Custard.
One day, Custard went for a walk in the forest and met a monkey. Then they met a big bad wolf.
"I don't like your colour," said the wolf.
The wolf was horrible. They started to fight but then the horse had a thought. When the wolf was asleep, Custard painted the wolf's skin blue so he could say he didn't like *his* colour. A farmer saw what was happening and went to help Custard.

Indah Taseseb
Little Dewchurch C of E Primary School, Little Dewchurch

ANIMAL FACTS

What elephants eat:
Elephants eat 17kg of vegetation.

How much they weigh:
Elephants weigh more than 100 people
They are eight tons

How big elephants are:
Elephants are the world's largest animal

How long baby elephants walk for:
Baby elephants can walk for an hour
But they are very shaky.

Toby Temperley (7)
Little Dewchurch C of E Primary School, Little Dewchurch

THE WILD WOLF AND THE HORSE

"Hello, you are funny!" said Horse.
"Do you want to be my friend?" asked Wolf.
"Yes, let's go play," replied Horse.
They trotted into the wood. Next, a woodcutter came and chopped down the trees. The animals were scared. They tricked the woodcutter and he ran far, far away.

Zac Crump (6)
Little Dewchurch C of E Primary School, Little Dewchurch

JAGUAR

J umps high in the sky
A stealthy spotted big cat just like a spy
G rowls angrily at its prey
U nattachable speed in the water where it should stay
A dorable cubs who sometimes weep
R iver swimming lovers in shallow and deep.

Alana Scanlon (7)
Little Dewchurch C of E Primary School, Little Dewchurch

TIGER

T errific pouncing
I ncredible black stripes
G rabbing with big furry paws
E xtremely good at climbing tall trees
R oars loudly across the ginormous jungle.

Amber (7)
Little Dewchurch C of E Primary School, Little Dewchurch

TIGER

T erribly strong
I ncredibly loud like a thunderbolt
G rowls strongly like a bell
E xtremely fast as jumping
R eally cute cubs like a teddy bear.

Ameilia McCormack (7)
Little Dewchurch C of E Primary School, Little Dewchurch

RAVENS

Did you know you can make a raven talk?
Ravens can have white necks
Ravens make eeee sounds
Cats eat and kill ravens
There are white ravens.

Leon Clarke (7)
Little Dewchurch C of E Primary School, Little Dewchurch

GIRAFFES FACT FILE

Giraffes are so tall they have to bend down
Giraffes eat tomatoes, salad, lettuce
Giraffes can kill lions with their big strong neck to strangle them.

Oliver Eames (7)
Little Dewchurch C of E Primary School, Little Dewchurch

CUCKOOS

There are 54 types of cuckoo
Cuckoos live in Africa, Asia and Australia
In England, a cuckoo was first seen in 1953.

Jack Ovel (6)
Little Dewchurch C of E Primary School, Little Dewchurch

THE FIERCE LION

The lion has a golden mane that sparkles in the sun
Sharp, shiny claws to scratch on trees to mark their territory
Yellow scary teeth that eat animals
Blonde fur to camouflage in the straw
Fierce eyes that look at their prey
They walk slowly to pounce on their prey
A pink twitchy nose to smell their food
Big paws to help them fight
Listening ears to hear their prey
Big legs to help them run.

Marion Hornik-Caly (7)
Northfield Primary School, South Kirkby

AWESOME ANIMALS - WONDERFUL WILDLIFE

THE GOLD FURRY LION

The mane is brown and golden in colour
Its mane is fluffier than anything on its body
It can roar five miles further than anything
I know
It stalks gazelle and zebra for its prey
It's at the top of the food chain for animals
Its enemy is a hyena and they fight all
the time
They get scars
They scratch and they roar
They have sharp claws to mark their territory.

Elouise Turner (7)
Northfield Primary School, South Kirkby

THE GREY BIG ELEPHANT

Two big grey ears to listen for creatures
A big mouth to gobble up food that is big
Has big feet to stomp loudly
So animals can hear it to warn them
That they are coming
A big trunk to squirt out water
Has big white tusks to kill predators
Has big baggy feet to trot for a long time.

Sophia Palochova (6)
Northfield Primary School, South Kirkby

A LION

A lion with sharp teeth.
A golden mane that shimmers in the light.
Huge sharp claws to mark their territory.
Yellow-stained teeth that devour their prey.
A lion's roar can be heard two miles away.
He eats deer, buffalo, chicken and zebra and anything that gets in his way.

Cody Tate (7)
Northfield Primary School, South Kirkby

THE FIERCE

A golden mane that shimmers in the light
Huge sharp claws to mark their territory
Yellow-stained teeth that devour their prey
Brown furry colour that helps them camouflage
It roars at night when everyone is fast asleep
Everyone thinks it is a wolf.

Julia Kosiur (7)
Northfield Primary School, South Kirkby

THE CUTE ZEBRA

Lake chugger
Straw demolisher
Plain walker
Grass grazer
Herd runner
Wasteland wanderer
Family lover
Protective parent
Leaf chomper
Large body
Large mouth
Huge legs
Black and white stripes
Cute zebra.

Jase Symonds (7)
Northfield Primary School, South Kirkby

THE LION

It devours meat when it is hungry
It has sharp claws to kill its prey
It has sharp claws to protect itself
It has a loud roar to make it sound dangerous
It has claws to mark its territory
It has yellow-stained teeth that gnaw on bones.

Mia Ikwu-Nowakawska (7)
Northfield Primary School, South Kirkby

THE SPOTTY GIRAFFE

They have a long neck to reach leaves on tall trees and lick wood
They have spots on their body to camouflage when in danger
Four unsteady legs to trot across the plain so they can get food
They have a thin neck so the food can slide down.

Caleb Stennett-Aspey (7)
Northfield Primary School, South Kirkby

THE GIRAFFE

Four long legs for walking on the plain
Has a long purple tongue
The plain stroller looking up high for leaves
Loves to eat leaves with its family
A long thin neck that helps them reach high leaves in the trees.

Leila Spencer (7)
Northfield Primary School, South Kirkby

AWESOME ANIMALS - WONDERFUL WILDLIFE

THE GIRAFFE

A tall thin neck to reach leaves on some trees
Four wobbly legs to walk across the plain
A stretchy purple tongue that licks wood
A spotty beige body to camouflage in the bushes
They lick their baby calves.

Jacob Hendson (6)
Northfield Primary School, South Kirkby

LION

A huge brown shaggy mane
That shimmers in the day
A huge rectangle body
An afternoon sleeper
A night-time roarer
A powerful brown strong body
A meat devourer
They stalk their prey.

Freddie Rawson (7)
Northfield Primary School, South Kirkby

WHAT AM I?

A kennings poem

Meat lover
Zebra catcher
Night-time stalker
Afternoon snorer
Fast runner
Pride lover
Furry mane
Vicious roarer
Sharp, vicious claws
A lion.

Jesse Jackson (7)
Northfield Primary School, South Kirkby

THE ROARING LION

The roaring lion sleeps in the daytime
His golden mane shimmers in the light
He has huge sharp claws to mark his territory
Yellow-stained teeth that devour his prey.

Freddie Laws (7)
Northfield Primary School, South Kirkby

GIRAFFE

Four wobbly legs to go across the plain
A dotty beige body to camouflage
A tall thin neck to eat leaves off the tree
A long purple tongue that licks the trees.

Olivia Hobson (7)
Northfield Primary School, South Kirkby

THE ROARING LION

A kennings poem

Bone crusher
Loud roarer
Afternoon dreamer
Meat lover
Prey hunter
Animal killer
Family protector
A lion.

Charlotte Clarke (6)
Northfield Primary School, South Kirkby

WHAT AM I?

A kennings poem

Meat lover
Night-time killer
Family lover
Fast runner
Hyena jumper
Zebra killer
A lion.

Hunter-James Gill (7)
Northfield Primary School, South Kirkby

DEADLY LION

A kennings poem

Hyena fighter
Meat devourer
Loud roarer
Human killer
Fast runner
Zebra chaser
A lion.

Finley Jennings (7)
Northfield Primary School, South Kirkby

THE TERRIFYING LION

A kennings poem

Wasteland prowler
Hyena fighter
Midnight stalker
Savannah killer
A lion.

Roman Playford (7)
Northfield Primary School, South Kirkby

WHAT AM I?
A kennings poem

Ear twitcher
Calf protector
Detecting stroller
Tongue roller
A giraffe.

George Williams (7)
Northfield Primary School, South Kirkby

WHAT AM I?

A kennings poem

Hyena fighter
Meat chomper
Afternoon snorer
Night-time pouncer
A lion.

Georgia Bedford (6)
Northfield Primary School, South Kirkby

WHAT AM I?

A kennings poem

Leaf gobbler
Neck stretcher
Savannah walker
Ear twitcher
A giraffe.

Ella Varley (7)
Northfield Primary School, South Kirkby

WHAT AM I?

A kennings poem

Meat predator
Hyena fighter
Territory marker
Animal hunter
A lion.

Xander Taylor (7)
Northfield Primary School, South Kirkby

GUESS THE ANIMAL

A kennings poem

Straw slopper
Savannah muncher
Lake slurper
Grass grazer
A zebra.

Kitty Gornall (7)
Northfield Primary School, South Kirkby

AWESOME ANIMALS - WONDERFUL WILDLIFE

WHAT AM I?

A kennings poem

Plain dasher
Lake chugger
Herd runner
Straw demolisher
A zebra.

Cameron Stuart (7)
Northfield Primary School, South Kirkby

THE LION
A kennings poem

Afternoon sleeper
Meat eater
Prey hunter
Animal killer
A lion.

Oscar Hampton (7)
Northfield Primary School, South Kirkby

WHAT AM I?

A kennings poem

Plain drinker
Straw sipper
Herd runner
Grass grazer
A zebra.

Blake Raboijane (7)
Northfield Primary School, South Kirkby

WHAT AM I?

A kennings poem

Lake traveller
African runner
Savannah trotter
Straw gobbler.

Eli John (7)
Northfield Primary School, South Kirkby

DUCKS IN DANGER

Once upon a time, there was a mummy duck and a baby duck having fun in the pond. Rose and Daisy were their names.
It was a summer day, nice and peaceful. Perfect blue sky, green grass and colourful flowers all around. Suddenly, a big crocodile came by looking for some food. A pair of evil eyes, big mouth and dangerous teeth approached.
"Oh no! Run, Daisy!" said Rose. "Before we are eaten!"
With a *quack, quack* and a flap of their wings, they asked for help.
"SOS! SOS!"
Soon three children appeared to the rescue. The children had some magical flowers that they threw into the mouth of the crocodile. In a few seconds, the crocodile turned into a sweet goldfish.

Chloe Meno Pena (6)
Pilgrim Primary Academy, Plymouth

THE LITTLE LAMB

One day, there was a little lamb. The little lamb had some friends. There was a panda that taught her to climb palm trees.
The next day, her bunny friend helped her to jump so high in the sky.
The next day, an animal rescuer caught the little lamb, the panda and the bunny. They were put into the back of a truck.
They were put into a cage for people to adopt them. The panda was adopted first, then the little lamb and the bunny.
They all went home with happy families.

Luna Williams (6)
Pilgrim Primary Academy, Plymouth

GARDEN KINGDOM

One day a cat jumped out of a window onto a tree. A ladybird fell out of the tree and hurt its wing. A snail helped the ladybird and carried it on its back. A butterfly saw and went to get a bandage. A bee saw and gave the ladybird some honey. A woodlouse saw them and found some shade for the ladybird to rest. The shade was a new home for all the new friends. The ladybird got better and stayed with the snail forever.

Fay Osborne (6)
Pilgrim Primary Academy, Plymouth

THE SCHOOL TRIP

A few months ago, I had the best day ever. I went to the farm on a school trip with my class. The sun was shining as bright as Mars. First, we had to get on the big coach. It was noisy and loud, but I didn't mind. It didn't take long to get there.

When we arrived we had to walk down a long thin lane to get to the noisy farm. When we finally got to the farm I was very excited. I couldn't wait to see all the cute animals. We put our bags down first in the cosy coffee house. Then we all set off on our adventure. First, I saw some cute fluffy meerkats looking up at me. They made me feel happy and smile. It was the best day ever.

Amy H (7)
Pontprennau Primary School, Pontprennau

AWESOME ANIMALS - WONDERFUL WILDLIFE

THE SCHOOL TRIP

A month ago, my class went to an amazing cool farm. First, I went to the busy loud bus, Next, my class arrived at the popular cool farm. After that, I saw some pretty colourful birds they were as cute as a puppy. Then I saw some funny, silly emus. They made me happy. I had a snack, I had some apples.

Soon after, I was so excited because I saw some very cute rabbits. I got lucky because I got to stroke some. Next, I got to see some hilarious horses. They made me even happier. After that, I had yummy lunch. Finally, I saw some cute little duckies. They quacked and quacked.

Cody Mitchell (7)
Pontprennau Primary School, Pontprennau

THE FARM TRIP

A few weeks ago, I went to the farm. The first thing we saw was the cute fluffy bunny rabbits. They were as cute as a baby. Then we saw a mummy peacock. She had laid her eggs and her babies hatched. Their cute cheeping beaks made me so happy. Then we saw some capybaras. An emu was chasing after it. It made me feel so excited. I wanted to go and see more animals. Finally, we went to pet some guinea pigs. Soon we went to feed some rabbits and then we had a snack.

Emily Vizard (7)
Pontprennau Primary School, Pontprennau

AWESOME ANIMALS - WONDERFUL WILDLIFE

THE FARM TRIP

In the month of June, we went to the farm. It was amazing. It was the best farm I ever went to. The sun was really bright. First, we saw rabbits. They were as cute as a puppy. I was super excited. Next, we went to the petting room. There were guinea pigs and rabbits. Then we saw the small meerkats and armadillos. We saw lots more animals. Then we had lunch. After lunch, we saw birds like peacocks and average birds.

Leo Moore (7)
Pontprennau Primary School, Pontprennau

THE SCHOOL TRIP

First, we went on a giant long bus. Next, we saw a fast animal. Then we saw a rabbit as cute as a baby lamb. Next, we saw some guinea pigs. They were so soft and lovely like a kitten.
After we had lunch in the warm, beautiful hut. For lunch, I had pasta, carrots and my water bottle. Finally, we went on the bus and went back to school. The parents picked up the children.

Neve Dunlop (7)
Pontprennau Primary School, Pontprennau

CHICKEN

C hickens are small, fluffy animals
H ide in the dark because they don't want to be bitten by a carnivore
I n the UK there are lots of white and black chickens
C hickens are cute lovely animals
K illing chickens gives you chicken which you eat
E veryone loves chicken
N oisy chickens cluck loudly.

Omer Mohamed
Pontprennau Primary School, Pontprennau

RABBITS

R abbits that are small, fluffy and jumping around like a frog
A rmadillos are as small as a rabbit
B rown bouncing sleepy rabbits
B ouncing black happy rabbits in the green field
I nside the cosy rabbit's hutch are lots of small rabbits
T iny white rabbits jumping all around in the green field.

Joshua Edwards (7)
Pontprennau Primary School, Pontprennau

DUCKS

D ucks are small, swimming creatures and love fish as feathery as a bird
U gly like the ugly duckling
C old water that they live in and the water is as cold as ice
K eep the happy, fluffy ducklings safe in the wet, blue pond.

Benjamin Andrews (7)
Pontprennau Primary School, Pontprennau

MEERKATS

M eerkats dig in the hard brown ground
E ating slimy bugs
E very meerkat likes hiding in the wood
R acing around as fast as a flash
K nife-like claws
A nnoying each other
T hey are very cute.

Noah Hammond
Pontprennau Primary School, Pontprennau

AWESOME ANIMALS - WONDERFUL WILDLIFE

FARM

F riendly animals running in their smelly cages
A rmadillos running playfully in light brown sand
R abbits are as soft as a blanket
M eerkats are as fluffy as a cat.

Akram Ahmed (7)
Pontprennau Primary School, Pontprennau

SHEEP

S heep have fluffy black and white wool
H ave you seen the sheep?
E ating the green grass
E veryone likes sheep
P et them on their big heads.

Emmanuel Okpan
Pontprennau Primary School, Pontprennau

HORSE

H ungry, lazy horse
O n a green bumpy field
R eady to eat horse food
S un shining in the distance
E veryone's favourite animal.

Eliana Eromhokhodion (7)
Pontprennau Primary School, Pontprennau

PIG

P igs are as smelly as an old sock
I n the mud, pigs roll
G o to the farm to see smelly messy and big pigs.

Hannah Van Keogh (7)
Pontprennau Primary School, Pontprennau

THE LOST MONKEY

Once upon a time, there was a family of monkeys who loved to explore and find food and shelter. One day, the monkey went out to find some food and got lost. The monkey saw an alligator and was shocked. He ran into a tiger and ran into a giraffe. He ran but then saw nothing. He found a tree and climbed it to hide. But no one came by the tree except his mum and dad. Then they lived happily ever after.

Emily Fletcher (7)
St Mary Cray Primary School, St Mary Cray

THE SLOTH WHO LOVES WATERMELON

Once upon a time far, far away was a sloth who loved watermelon.
One day when the sloth, named Flash, was hunting for watermelon, she found a gold watermelon. Flash opened the watermelon with her hand and found 7 gold pearls. Flash was very happy and she told her mum.

Tilly Sullivan (7)
St Mary Cray Primary School, St Mary Cray

AWESOME ANIMALS - WONDERFUL WILDLIFE

SUPER SPANIEL

Once in Redbourn, Super Spaniel was having his belly rubbed when... *clong!* A hazelnut hit the window. When he looked he saw Mega Squirrel smiling meanly at him. Super Spaniel was so furious that he teleported on Mega Squirrel's mean, ugly face. Mega Squirrel screamed in pain. Super Spaniel tried to whack the nut gun out of his furry paw but Mega Squirrel's grip was too strong. Suddenly, like a speeding bullet, Mega Squirrel clicked a button on his hand and a huge robot hazelnut jumped out of a tree trunk and fired a laser.
Luckily, Super Spaniel did not take too much damage. For some reason, Super Spaniel started whacking Mega Squirrel with his ears! But Mega Squirrel took no damage. Super Spaniel managed to hack the robot hazelnut so that was the end of that. But Super Spaniel still had to deal with Mega Squirrel.

Super Spaniel had an irresistible plan. He threw a stuffed bird over Mega Squirrel's head and he had no choice but to chase it. Whilst he chased it, Super Squirrel rammed into Mega Squirrel and blasted him away to the other side of the planet. "Yippee!" woofed Super Spaniel.
Super Spaniel saved the day!

Milo Glass (9)
St Nicholas CE (VA) Primary School, Harpenden

AN ANIMAL ADVENTURE

Wow! What an amazing day. It started like any other day. I was walking to collect a bit of grass and crunchy red prickly leaves. I could feel red damp crunchy leaves. The cats and birds were singing really loudly.

When I was walking home, the cold breeze was putting my fur up and my paws were getting wet by the damp grass. My black nose twitched by the cold breeze. My tail wagged because when I had eaten my tea, I could go to sleep. I jumped with joy.

Suddenly, I heard a meowing noise. The strange sound was coming from a tall tree. When it noticed me it started coming out slowly. When it got to the middle it jumped out and walked closer and stared. Then it started hissing. I barked. The cat was scared and it ran away.

After that, I got some grass and went home to eat. I felt really tired so after that I went to bed.

Eliza Williamson (7)
The Manor CE Primary School, Coalpit Heath

AN ANIMAL ADVENTURE

Wow! What a mysterious day! In front of my eyes were the trunks of trees.

Going hunting from prey to prey, eating meat all day. My scratching claws were as sharp as knives and all this delicious food will be mine.

As the leaves crunched underneath my feet, I saw shaking bushes around me. The blasting wind zoomed, brushing my long fur and the fish that came from the lake were making a disgusting smell.

While I was walking along, I spotted a weird patch of light green grass and I felt curious. I walked over the patch of grass and fell through it into a deep cave. Luckily, there was a river at the bottom and I dropped into it. I started panicking because I'd fallen into the centre of the river so I swam out.

As soon as I got out, I hunted for an exit but suddenly, I spotted that my family had fallen down too. We helped each other get out and we all felt happy again.

On the way home, my family and I saw another patch of weird grass and we all fell down it. This time we landed on the other side of the river. We landed right next to a pack of wolves and we started to fight.

AWESOME ANIMALS - WONDERFUL WILDLIFE

When it ended, I realised my family had won so we helped each other to find a way out. We found an exit and ended up getting home.

Teddy Pearce (7)
The Manor CE Primary School, Coalpit Heath

AN ANIMAL ADVENTURE

Wow! What a weird day. I was slithering along the forest floor when I saw a great big python. Then I saw a spider so I raced to it but he ate it up like nothing.

I heard loud, crunchy leaves. Then I smelled a stale smell. It smelt disgusting. I slithered, I hissed. I waited. I'm fast. I'm deadly. I flashed out and caught my prey.

Suddenly, I heard a rattling noise coming from the bushes. I looked around and saw an orange predator coming out from the bushes. It had sharp teeth and he was fierce. It was a massive fox. I bit his foot, he was crying in pain. Then he watched me run far, far away.

I got some food because I was hungry. Then another fox came out from the undergrowth then it chased after me because I poisoned the other one but he couldn't catch me. But he did scratch me in a lot of places. I was bleeding in a lot of places. I was crying because it really hurt. Lots of the pythons were checking if I was okay. I was not okay. I was crying out loud because it really hurt. There was blood everywhere but I did get food in the end.

Teddy Luton (7)
The Manor CE Primary School, Coalpit Heath

AN ANIMAL ADVENTURE

Wow! What an amazing day. I am resting in an African grassy and muddy plain. I love to run and chase my fast prey and eat it
while it is fresh. I am the fastest animal on Earth. I have giant paws. The cold breeze made me feel nice, from boiling hot to medium temperature. Suddenly, a gazelle started to chase me. I ran but I wasn't careful and I ran into the deep woods. I was lost in the cold woods. I solved the problem by going out the way I came in. Then after I was out of the damp woods, I killed the gazelle and just as I was going to eat it, I heard a *thud, thud, thud*. It came through the bushes and it stood on my beautiful tail. I yelped and ran into the wet woods. I was lost.
"Oopsy doopsy!" I said.
It started all over again.
"Oh no!" I said.

Benjamin Scopes (7)
The Manor CE Primary School, Coalpit Heath

AN ANIMAL ADVENTURE

Wow! What a freezing day! The icy snowflakes were falling on my soft fur. I heard the breeze flowing by me. The dead trees were blowing in the wind and the snow was fiercely attacking the landscape. My paws were numb and freezing. "Achoo! I think I might need to find shelter." Suddenly, a loud roar came behind from a huge iceberg. A predator had arrived. It had huge paws, black eyes and rough fur. It was a polar bear. The polar bear began to chase me all over the place. Finally, I saw a snowy mountain in the distance. I ran and ran. I didn't even look behind me. I hid behind the mountain and the polar bear had no idea. The polar bear gave up and went home.
I went back to my icy, frosty cave and went to sleep as the moonlight shone.

Sebastian Milkins (7)
The Manor CE Primary School, Coalpit Heath

AN ANIMAL ADVENTURE

Wow! What an amazing day. Today I began my day by playing with noisy fluffy bees. Ow! I got stung. I smelt bright pink flowers. "Achoo! Achoo! Bless me!"
I looked down at my small fluffy paws. "Oh, a mouse. I'm gonna catch it."
Suddenly, a dog came out of a cat flap. It was brown and it had blue eyes. It picked me up and threw me on the ground. I hissed and scratched his eye. He ran away crying in pain.
"Achoo! Achoo!"
"Awooo! Grrr!"
A wolf helped pick me up. *Zzzz!* I fell asleep. All of a sudden, I was lost in a deep dark forest. I was scared.

Robin Neesam (7)
The Manor CE Primary School, Coalpit Heath

AWESOME ANIMALS - WONDERFUL WILDLIFE

AN ANIMAL ADVENTURE

Wow! What a sunny day. I was flying up in the bright blue sky. I swooped down into the dark blue ocean and I soared back up into the bright blue sky. I could see my fluffy red feathers floating around the fresh air.

All of a sudden, a strange noise in the green bushes and all of the fresh leaves started to fall from the green bush. Suddenly, a yellow lion appeared with red eyes and sharp teeth. When the lion tried to run, he tripped over a brown log. The lion ran away so I ran away as well.

"No! No!" I said. "I went the wrong way!"

Karson Wong (7)
The Manor CE Primary School, Coalpit Heath

AN ANIMAL ADVENTURE

Wow! What a wonderful day. It was a normal day hunting tasty rabbits to eat. I heard brown, crunchy leaves. I felt a cold relaxing breeze. I could smell freshly cut grass and I could smell something tasty. I have a furry body and big grey paws. I also have four legs. I creep quickly around.
A white furry rabbit appeared from some green bushes. I chased the tasty rabbit. The rabbit jumped over a deep damp hole. I fell into the hole with a thump. The rabbit started eating carrots but a fox was waiting to eat her.

Kayden Smith (7)
The Manor CE Primary School, Coalpit Heath

AN ANIMAL ADVENTURE

Wow! What a scary day. The day began like this... I was wandering in the warm forest when some other animals were scattering in the tall trees. I was feeding my cute babies. They were eating bamboo. All of a sudden, one of the babies fell out of the tree. I went down to see if it was there but it had run off. I went to the end of the forest and saw an orange creature with black stripes. It was a tiger. It tried to attack my baby. I popped out and grabbed my baby. I took it back and carried on eating bamboo.

Charlotte Britton (7)
The Manor CE Primary School, Coalpit Heath

AN ANIMAL ADVENTURE

It was a great day. I was swimming through the seawater when I saw some fish. The nice sea water was touching me all the time. I heard some waves above me and I could smell the air above me too. I had really sharp teeth and I ate fish. I could breathe in the water. Suddenly, something bad happened.
I got stuck in a shipwreck and I didn't know what to do. But then I had an idea. With my sharp teeth, I bit the shipwreck ten times. Then, to end the day, I ate some fish.

James Martin (7)
The Manor CE Primary School, Coalpit Heath

AN ANIMAL ADVENTURE

Wow! What a beautiful day. I feel white and brown bamboo. I can smell lollipops. I can hear birds tweeting. I love eating bamboo but I also love climbing. Bamboo is my breakfast.
All of a sudden, I hear a weird sound coming from a bush. It comes out and peers at me. I peer back. It is grey and its nose is black.
"Achoo! My nose is allergic to grass. I have to put a mask on!"
I run as fast as I can but it is faster than me.

Samira Kaur-Clark (7)
The Manor CE Primary School, Coalpit Heath

AN ANIMAL ADVENTURE

Wow! What a beautiful day. After I ate my bananas, I went to the park. I went on the swings and I went on the slides. When I was at the park, there was a mysterious predator growling at me.
"Roar! I am a fierce predator," said the predator, "I am going to eat you."
"I am going to hunt you now," I said with a cheeky smile on my face.
I jumped off the tree branch and landed right on his belly.

Niomi Denning (7)
The Manor CE Primary School, Coalpit Heath

AN ANIMAL ADVENTURE

Wow! What a cool day. It started as a normal day in the warm rainforest. I felt the short grass and the cold breeze. I heard the slow wind and a lion roar. I saw dirty bugs but I ate rats and mice. Suddenly, a fierce red and yellow lion popped up from behind and started chasing me. I slithered over the grass, logs and concrete. I jumped into the water to save myself because I'm a good swimmer and I started laughing at the lion.

Grayson McLauchlin (7)
The Manor CE Primary School, Coalpit Heath

AN ANIMAL ADVENTURE

Wow! What a cold day. In front of me, there was cold lovely meat. When I took a nibble of the meat, it made my ferocious, bloody mouth cold.
Up above, birds were tweeting but I couldn't climb trees because my claws weren't sharp enough. Luckily, the birds swooped down and I took a big bite out of them. It was super fun. I took the birds back to my family.

River Amott (7)
The Manor CE Primary School, Coalpit Heath

AN ANIMAL ADVENTURE

Wow! What a beautiful day. I could see lollipop trees and heart flowers and I jumped in a pile of leaves. Suddenly, a wolf stared at me. I pounced on the lollipop trees and the wolf followed me. Then I saw a pile of leaves. I ran to the pile of leaves and ran and ran. I was tired and kept running. I finally got there and the wolf could not find me.

Neve Wood (7)
The Manor CE Primary School, Coalpit Heath

AN ANIMAL ADVENTURE

Wow! What a beautiful day.

On a sunny morning, a spider was on the dirt. I was crawling on the dirt and I could hear yaps outside. The person! It was crawling towards me. It was getting closer. Then the person went the other way. I just kept running and running. I saw him in the distance and I climbed a tree. I then couldn't see him.

Thomas Tovey (7)
The Manor CE Primary School, Coalpit Heath

AWESOME ANIMALS - WONDERFUL WILDLIFE

MY HORSE, DEZZY

My horse, Dezzy, looks like a snow tiger
My horse, Dezzy, sounds like *neigh, neigh, neigh*
My horse, Dezzy, feels very, very fluffy
My horse, Dezzy, smells like sweet hay
He makes me feel safe.

Tomas Price (7)
Trerobart Primary School, Ynysybwl

MY DOG

My dog looks like a tiger
My dog sounds like *woof, woof*
My dog feels like a teddy
My dog tastes like perfume
My dog smells like beef
He makes me feel excited.

Cooper Kingsbury-James (7)
Trerobart Primary School, Ynysybwl

MY DOG, MATEO

My dog looks like a ghost
My dog sounds like a small dog
My dog feels like rough skin
My dog likes the taste of pizza
My dog smells like mud
He makes me feel excited.

Sophia Belle Rees (6)
Trerobart Primary School, Ynysybwl

MY DOG

My dog looks like a cwtchy, spotty cushion
My dog sounds like *bark, bark*
My dog feels like a fluffy blanket
My dog smells like wet grass
He makes me feel relaxed.

Niall Binks (7)
Trerobart Primary School, Ynysybwl

FISH

My fish looks gold
My fish sounds like *puh, puh, puh*
My fish feels slimy
My fish tastes like cheese
My fish smells like strawberries
He makes me feel safe.

Addison Powell (6)
Trerobart Primary School, Ynysybwl

MY DOG

My dog looks like a zebra
My dog sounds sad
My dog feels like fluffy clouds
My dog tastes sweet like sweets
My dog smells awesome
She makes me feel relaxed.

Salvador Ribeiro (6)
Trerobart Primary School, Ynysybwl

MY DOG

My dog looks cute
My dog sounds like *woof*
My dog feels like pom-poms
My dog tastes like fur
My dog smells like dirt
He makes me feel happy.

Mila McIntosh (6)
Trerobart Primary School, Ynysybwl

MY DOG

My dog looks like a rat
My dog sounds like a bark
My dog feels like a pom-pom
My dog tastes like fur
My dog smells like mud
He makes me feel fuzzy.

Theodore Nalej (7)
Trerobart Primary School, Ynysybwl

THE SNAKE

I can see a venomous snake
I can hear hissing
I can feel it following me
I can smell chicken nuggets.

Bobby Nutland (6)
Trerobart Primary School, Ynysybwl

MIKE'S PEPPERONI PIZZA

Once upon a time, there lived a gorilla called Mike. Mike was different from all the other gorillas as Mike preferred to eat pizza than bananas. Mike was the biggest gorilla in the London Zoo. Each day at 3pm, Mike would beat his chest loud enough for the local pizzeria to hear and they would deliver five pepperoni pizzas. All the other animals were jealous of Mike's pizza.
One day, they asked Mike to share his pizza. Mike agreed and continued to share his pizza with the other animals each day. He enjoyed the company and of course, sharing with his friends.

Jude McKellow (7)
Vane Road Primary School, Newton Aycliffe

BESTIES

Once, there was a dog called Lilly. She loved her owner, Amelia. They did everything together. Amelia loved to give Lilly a bath. Once she was nice and clean she would dry Lilly and then put a beautiful sparkly bow in her hair. They played catch in the garden and then she took Lilly for a long walk.

They went home, had food and snuggled on the couch watching a movie. They ended up falling asleep.

Amelia Wingfield (6)
Vane Road Primary School, Newton Aycliffe

KEEP THE CATS SAFE

A girl called Farah had a ginger cat named Haimish. One day something terrible happened. The cat went missing. Luckily, Haimish was microchipped. Farah's best friend, Lily, found him and took him to the vet. The microchip showed the cat was owned by Farah.

Teddy (7)
Vane Road Primary School, Newton Aycliffe

YOUNG WRITERS INFORMATION

We hope you have enjoyed reading this book – and that you will continue to in the coming years.

If you're the parent or family member of an enthusiastic poet or story writer, do visit our website **www.youngwriters.co.uk/subscribe** and sign up to receive news, competitions, writing challenges and tips, activities and much, much more! There's lots to keep budding writers motivated!

If you would like to order further copies of this book, or any of our other titles, then please give us a call or order via your online account.

Young Writers
Remus House
Coltsfoot Drive
Peterborough
PE2 9BF
(01733) 890066
info@youngwriters.co.uk

Join in the conversation!
Tips, news, giveaways and much more!

YoungWritersUK   YoungWritersCW
youngwriterscw   youngwriterscw